AF256040

When Will My **Flowers** Bloom?

A Springtime Picture Book About Patience and Growing in Your Own Time

By Abyy Sparklewood

🌼 About The Blooming Hearts Collection

The Blooming Hearts Collection is a series of gentle, uplifting picture books that help children understand big feelings in simple, beautiful ways.

Each book explores themes like:

- Patience
- Confidence
- Kindness
- Friendship
- Growing at your own pace

These stories remind children that every heart blooms differently — and that's what makes each one special.

More Blooming Hearts adventures are on the way!

Lina stood at the edge of her yard, watching Mrs. Alvarez's garden sway in the breeze.
Pink tulips reached tall and proud. Golden daffodils nodded in the sunshine.

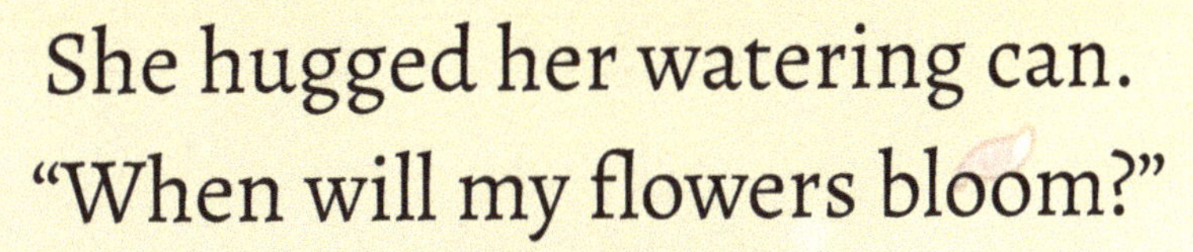

She hugged her watering can.
"When will my flowers bloom?"

That afternoon, she planted her seeds in careful rows.
She tucked each tiny seed into the soil like a treasure.

"Grow big," she whispered.
"Grow bright."

The next morning, Lina ran outside barefoot.

She knelt down.
She leaned close.
She waited. Brown dirt.
Nothing else.

Across the fence, petals
opened wider.
The tulips seemed taller.
The daffodils seemed brighter.

Lina pressed her fingers
gently into her soil.
Still quiet. Still still.

Day after day, she watered
and watched.

She tilted her head.
She squinted at the earth.
"Why is it taking so long?" she sighed.

One afternoon, Lina brushed the
top of the soil.
"Are you broken?" she whispered.
The garden did not answer.

Across the fence, petals
fluttered and danced.

"Gardens grow in their own time," Grandma said gently. "Before flowers show themselves to the sun, they grow strong underneath."

"Underneath?" Lina asked.
"In the dark," Grandma nodded.
"Roots stretch and reach and hold on tight."
Lina imagined tiny roots twisting deep below her feet.

The next morning, Lina picked up her watering can again.
Not because she saw green.
Not because she saw buds.

But because she believed something was happening
where she couldn't see.

Days passed.
The tulips across the fence began to fade.

Lina bent low one quiet morning—
and gasped.
A small green curve pushed
through the soil.

It wasn't tall.
It wasn't bright.
But it was brave.
Lina smiled.

"You weren't broken,"
she whispered.

Weeks later, petals opened wide toward the sky. Lina stood beside her blooming garden, sunlight warming her cheeks.

"When will my flowers bloom?" she thought.
They bloom in their own time.
And so do I.
The End.

About the Author 🌸

Abyy Sparklewood is a children's book author who loves creating gentle stories that inspire kindness, patience, and emotional growth. Through her Blooming Hearts Collection, she hopes to help young readers learn important life lessons while discovering the beauty of nature and the joy of believing in themselves.

When she isn't writing stories, Abyy enjoys spending time with family, exploring creative projects, and finding inspiration in the simple wonders of everyday life.

🌼 **Did you and your child enjoy this story?** 🌸

If When Will My Flowers Bloom? brought a smile to your child's face, I would be so grateful if you left a short review on Amazon.

Reviews help other families discover stories that inspire patience, kindness, and believing in their own time to bloom.

Your support also helps independent authors like me continue creating meaningful stories for young readers.

Even a sentence or two makes a big difference.

Thank you for reading and being part of this journey.

With gratitude,
Abyy Sparklewood

 Author of the Blooming Hearts CollectionMore stories are growing soon in the Blooming Hearts Collection. 🌱

Leave a review on Amazon

🌷 A Little Gift for You

Did your child enjoy this story?

I created a FREE Spring Activity Pack inspired by When Will My Flowers Bloom?

Inside you'll find:

🌼 A spring coloring page

🌸 A flower dot-to-dot

🐝 A "Help the bunny Find the carrot" maze

Each activity gently reminds children:

We all bloom in our own time.

Download your free printable at:

abyysparklewood.com/spring-activity-pack/

Or scan the QR code below.

More Blooming Hearts Collection adventures are coming soon.

Keep blooming. 🌸

— Abyy Sparklewood

ALSO BY
ABYY SPARKLEWOOD

www.amazon.com/author/beautyinbooks-for kidsandadults

www.amazon.com/author/beautyinbooks

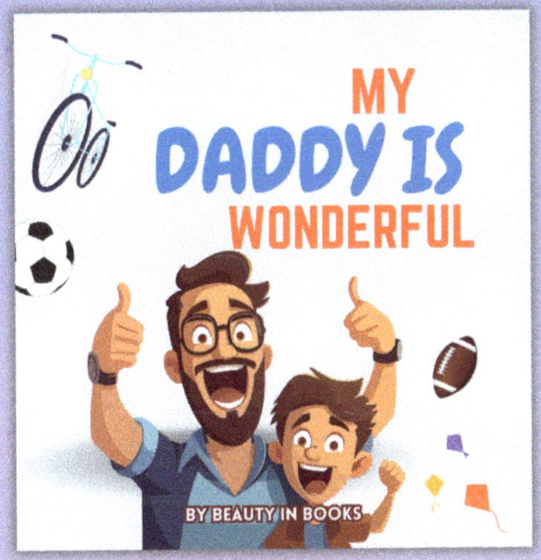

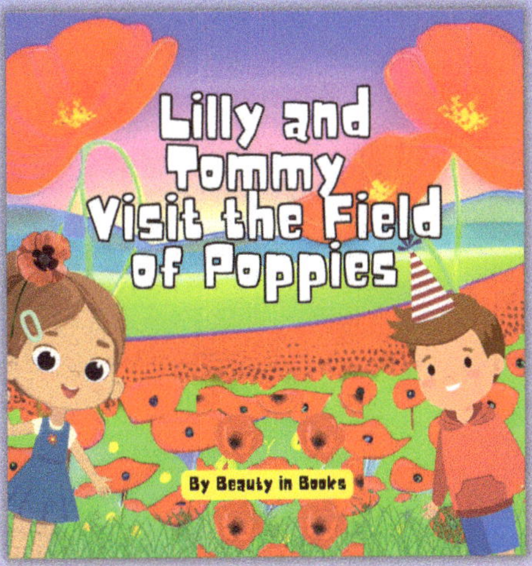

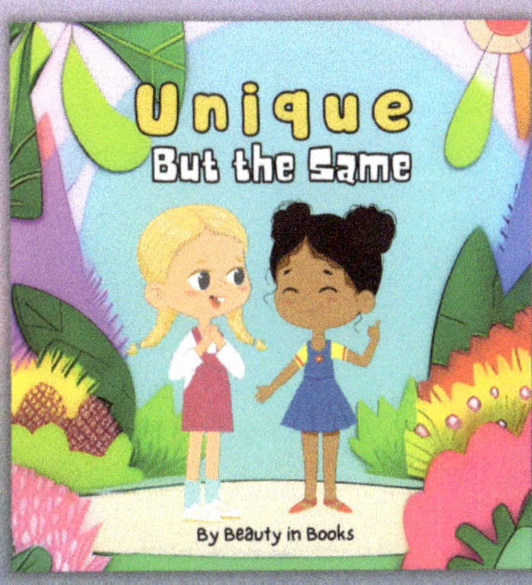

Thank you for reading!

 This book is part of The Blooming Hearts Collection, a series created to help little ones grow with courage, kindness, and confidence.

 Look out for more books in the Blooming Hearts Collection. 🌸

9 781961 634916